SHORT VOWEL

Silly
Sentences

Written by:
Arianne Simkus and Barbara Simkus

Illustrated by:
Barbara Simkus

Published by
The Paradigm Company
3500 Mountain View Dr.   Boise, ID, 83704   (208) 322-4440

Al can bat. Can Jack
bat? Mack and Jack
can bat.

Can Pat bat? Pat can
bat.

A NOTE TO PARENTS:

When reading with your child, please be patient.
You can not expect the child to know something
he or she has not been taught. It takes a lot of
repetition of the sounds for it to become firmly
entrenched in the child's hearing and seeing.

When the child comes to a word that is giving
difficulty, ask the child to sound it out with you
and say the word. If the child is letting you do the
sounding alone do it once and then have them
sound it out alone. Always keep a pleasant tone
in your voice.

Do not scold! If you feel yourself getting frus-
trated stop the reading and come back when you
are calm.

Repetition is the key. Hearing, saying, seeing and
writing will work wonders. Do not become con-
cerned if your child seems not to be able to get a
certain sound. Just keep saying and sounding it
out. Soon your child will ask you to stop and
want to do it alone.

Addendum to Set of Readers:
To assist in knowing which reader to use with which
lessons please use the following guide:

For: Alpha-Phonics:	For: How To Tutor:
Reader:	Reader:
1. Short Vowel A: Lessons 1-14	1. Short Vowel A: Lessons 1-9
2. Short Vowel E: Lessons 15-18	2. Short Vowel E: Lessons 10-12
3. Short Vowel I: Lessons 19-22	3. Short Vowel I: Lessons 13-17
4. Short Vowel O: Lessons 23-26	4. Short Vowel O: Lessons 18-19
5. Short Vowel U: Lessons 27-28	5. Short Vowel U: Lessons 20-22
6. The Chums: Lessons 29-33	6. The Chums: Lessons 23-30
7. Velvet The Cat: Lessons 42-48	7. Velvet The Cat: Lessons 31-42
8. The Big Fish: Lessons 49-56	8. The Big Fish: Lessons 43-49
9. The Contest: Lessons 57-76	9. The Contest: Lessons 50-57
10. Silly Sentences II: Lesson 77 +	10. Silly Sentences II: Lesson 58-71

Pam had a hat.

Dan had a hat
and a mat.

Zack had a hat, a
mat, and a bat.

Nat had a hat, a mat,
a bat and a fat cat .
Sam had a hat, a mat,
a bat, a fat cat, and a
rat.
Pat had a hat, a mat,
a bat, a fat cat, a rat
and a yak .

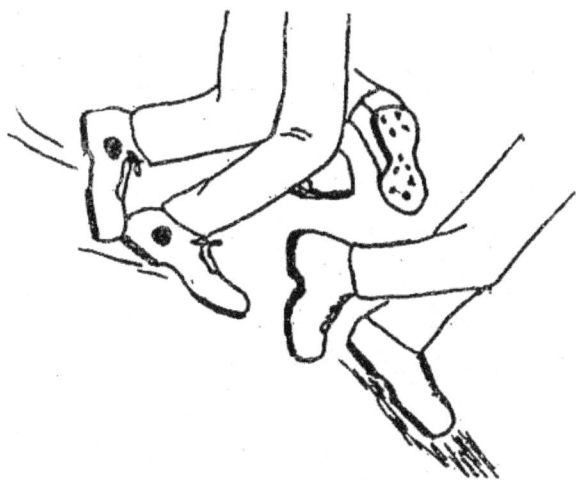

Yaz ran at Mack.
Mack ran at Cal.
Cal ran at Hal .
Hal ran at Jan.
Jan ran at Pam.
Can Pam tag Jack ?

Can a lap sag?
Can a cat bat?
Can a pack rat back
pack?
Can a yak, yack and
gab?
Can a gal quack?

Val has jam.
Mack has ham.
Was ham and jam
bad?
A hand can tap a map.
Can a map tap a
hand?

Jan has a fan.
Sal has a tan.
Dad has a van.
Mat has a can.
Tad has a pan.

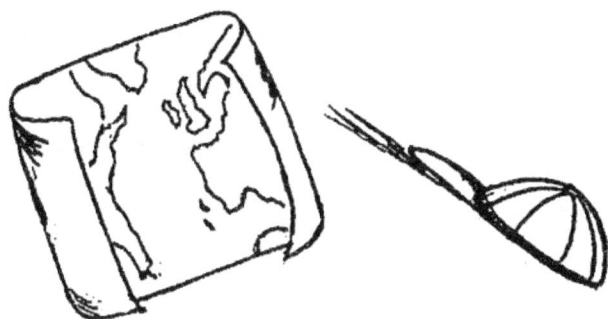

Dan has a map.

Tad has a map and
a cap.

Nat has a map, a
cap and a nap.

Was a fat cat at hand?

A fat cat had a sack.

Jab, jab at a bag was fat cat.

Fat cat had a nap.

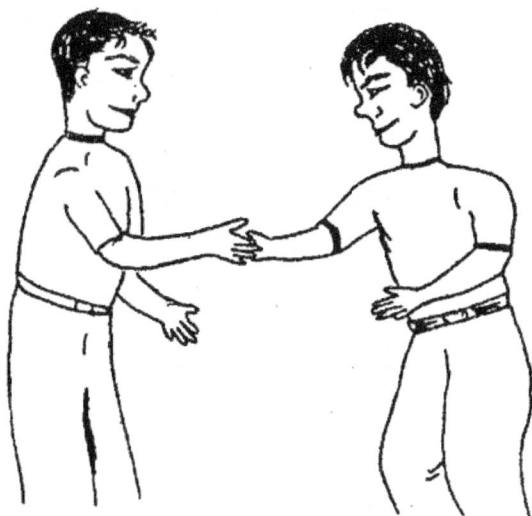

Mack has a pal.
Nat has a pal.
Nat was a bad lad.
Mack was mad at
Nat.
Mad, bad, sad!

Jack has a bag.

Cal has a rag.

Sal has a bag, a rag and a tag.

Can a rag tag a bag?

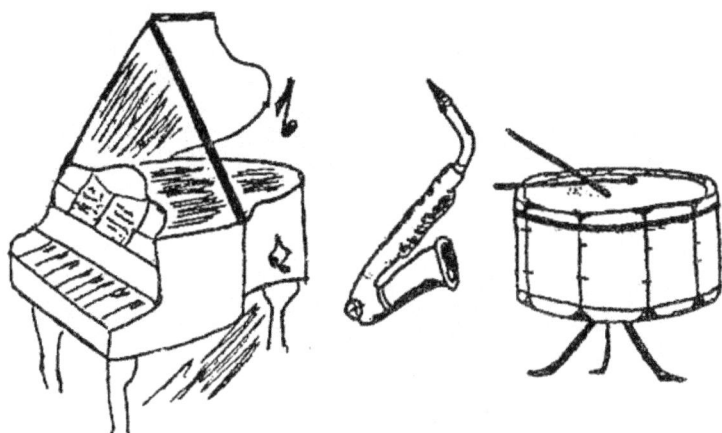

Max has a rag band.
Zack has a jazz
band.

Can a jazz band and
a rag band rap and
tap ?

SHORT VOWEL $\boxed{E}$

The Hen
and
The Pen

Written by:
Barbara Simkus

Illustrated by:
Barbara and Valerie Simkus

Published by
The Paradigm Company
3500 Mountain View Dr.   Boise, ID, 83704

Deb has a red hen.

The hen has a pen.

Tell Deb the hen
has an egg.

1

Deb can tend the
hen. Deb fed the
red hen.

Peck, peck, the red
hen fed.

2

Meg and Deb pet
the hen.

Meg has a cat.
The cat met the
hen. The hen ran
back. The cat
sat.

3

Dad let Meg get
an egg.

Deb had an egg
and Meg had an
egg.

Deb and Meg
gab.

Jeff and Ed sat at the pen.

The pen had a gap. The red hen ran at the gap.

5

Get a bag! Nab
the hen!

Jeff had a sack.
Ed had a net.

Jeff and Ed yell.

Meg and Deb tell
Dad.

Dad was mad and
yelled, "Get the
hen!"

Deb, Meg, Jeff,
Ed and Dad ran
and ran. The red
hen ran.

7

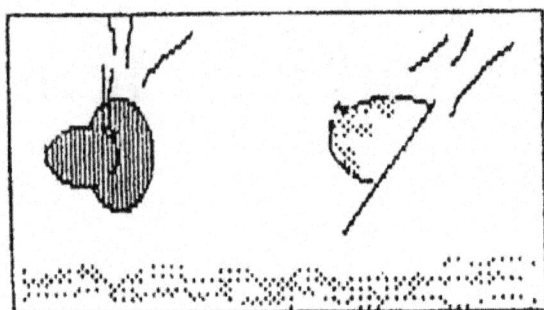

A hat fell. A cap
fell.

The hen ran and
ran. Dad ran at the
hen.

Get the net!

Get the sack!

The cat met the
hen!

Ed had the net.

Dad ran at the cat.

Let the net nab the cat.

10

Deb and Meg ran
at the hen.

Jeff had a sack.

The red hen ran
at the sack.

Jeff had the hen.

Ed had the cat.

Dad can mend the pen.

SHORT VOWEL $\boxed{\text{I}}$

TIM the PIG

Written by: Barbara Simkus
Illustrated by: Barbara & Valerie
Simkus

Published by
The Paradigm Company
3500 Mountain View Dr.   Boise, ID, 83704

Phil had a big pig.

The pig was in the pen.

Tim , the pig, was tan.

1

Phil had a big tin pan.

Phil will fill the pan.

Tim will get a bath.

Tim hid .

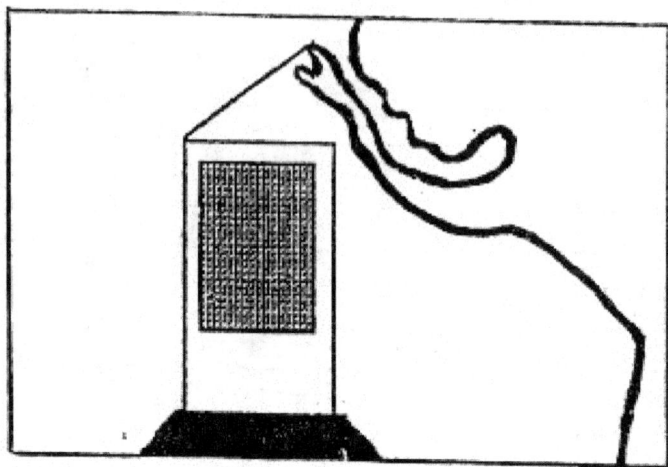

That pig has Phil in a
fix.

In the pen? In the
keg?

In the bin with the
lid? Tip it!

Tim was quick.

Then Tim did kick.

Phil did a zig and a zag.

Tim ran. Phil will
nab him.

In the bath with the
pig!

Phil is wet.

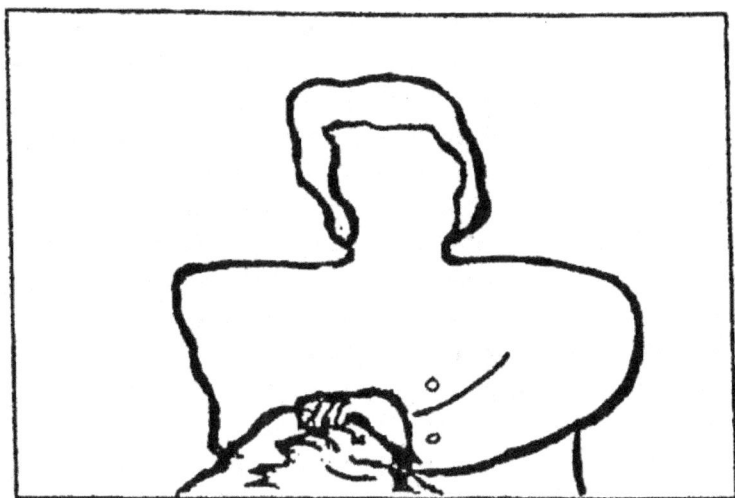

Phil will dip the rag
with his hand.

This pig was a mess.

Phil did dip till Tim
was red.

That big pig was a
gem.

Phil let Tim sit in the
path.

7

Then Phil let Tim

back in the pen.

Tim was wet.

Was Tim mad ?

8

Tim sat a bit in the pen.

Phil was in the den.

Then Tim sat in the sand.

It was wet.

Then Tim did dig.

Tim is tan.

The pig did a jig.

SHORT VOWEL $\boxed{O}$

Ron
and
Bob

Written and Illustrated by
Barbara Simkus

Published by
The Paradigm Company
3500 Mountain View Dr.   Boise, ID, 83704

The big mill sits on a
hill.

Bob and Ron ran on
the path.

The path led them on
the hill.

1

Bob got on top of a log.

Ron sat on a rock.

Ron has a map.

The map was of the

mill.

Dots on the map led

into the mill.

Bob and Ron hop off

the log and the rock.

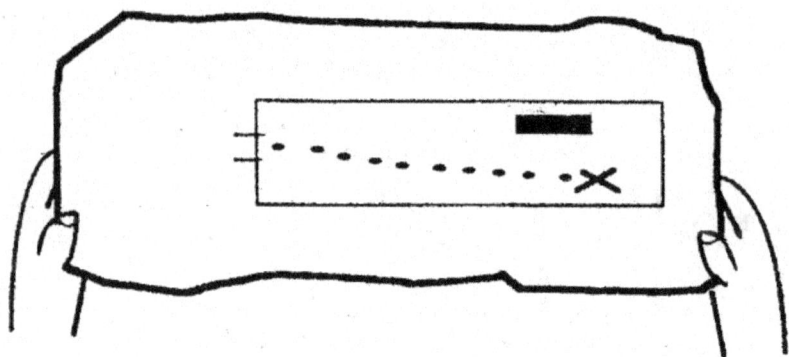

The mill did not lock.

Fog was on the land.

In the mill it was dim.

On the map , ten dots
then a red X.

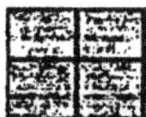

Ron fell in a pit.

A dog ran at Bob!

Bob did a zig and a zag.

" This is bad !" yells Bob.

5

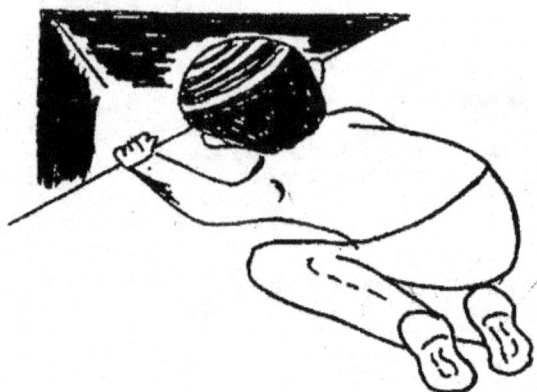

"Quick, " yells Ron,

"get Mom and Dad!"

Bob, with a nod, ran

and ran.

Bob tells Mom that

Ron is in a pit at the

mill.

Mom tells Dad.

At the mill , Ron gets

on top of a box.

His hand can not fit

on the rim of the pit.

8

Bob led Mom and
Dad in the mill.

Dad got a rod.

Ron's hand can fit on

the rod.

Dad and Bob get Ron
on top of the pit.

Then mom kisses
Ron.

Bob and Ron fill in
the pit with sod.

Dad tells Ron and
Bob that the map is
bad.

Mom and Dad lock
the mill.

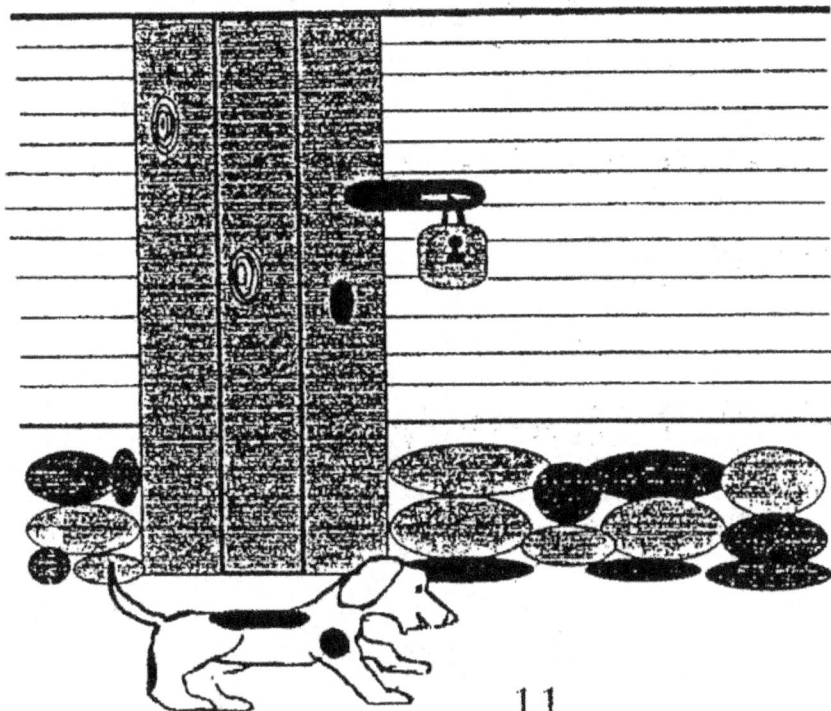

SHORT VOWEL $\boxed{U}$

PUG THE PUP

Written by:
Barbara Simkus

Illustrated by:
Valerie Simkus

Published by
The Paradigm Company
3500 Mountain View Dr.   Boise, ID, 83704

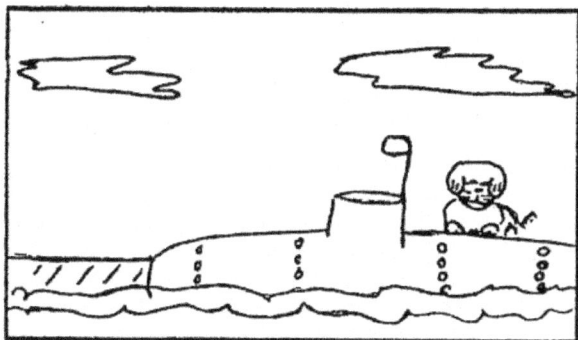

Pug is a pup. Pug tends a sub.

The sub is at a dock. The men will fix it.

The sun is hot. Pug is on the sub and has a nap.

Gill the gull sits on the sub.
Then Gill sits on Pug. Peck,
Peck, the gull pulls on Pug.
Pug is up and runs. Gill the
gull hops on the dock. Pug
is mad and yaps at Gill.

The gull is up, up, and lands on the sand.

Pug sits on the dock. A man has a rod and gets a cod.

Pug is full of pep. Pug tugs at the cod. The man pulls it back.

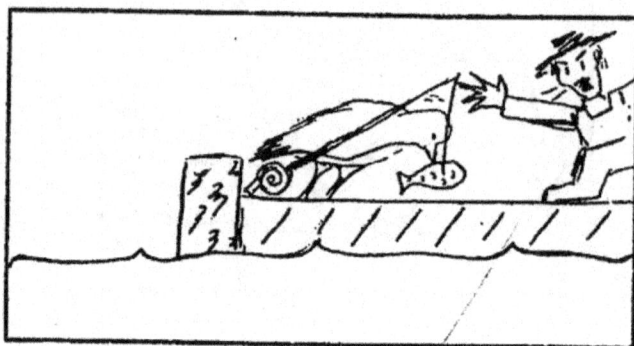

Gill is on the sand and hops on a jug.

Tug, Tug, and it tips. The jug is not full.

The gull is off and lands on the man's rod. Gill pecks at the cod.

The man is mad and runs at the gull.

Pug is on the dock and has a
nap.

The gull lands on Pug.

Peck, Peck, Gill tugs on

Pug. Pug is up.

Pug runs and tells Gill,

"Yap, Yap!"

The gull hops on the hull of

the sub.

5

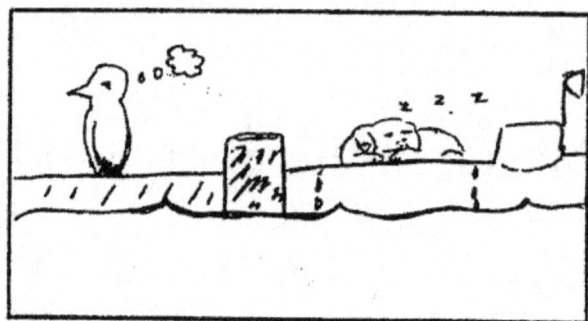

This is Pug's sub. Gill can

not sit on the sub. "Quit,

Quit!" yaps Pug.

Pug is on the sub. Gill zips

back on the dock.

Pug wags and has a nap.

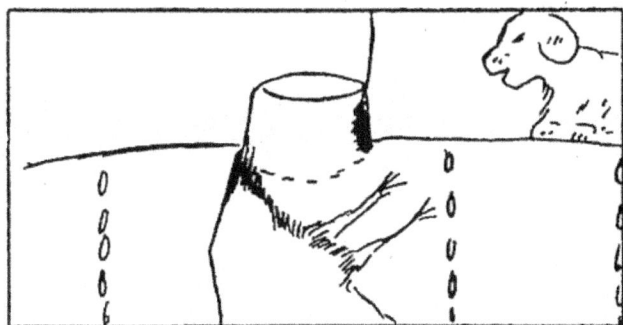

Up on the sub wends the
gull. Hop. Sit. Hop sit,
HOP! Gill is on Pug.
Tug, pull, peck! Pug is up
and mad. Pug is quick!
NIP! NIP!

7

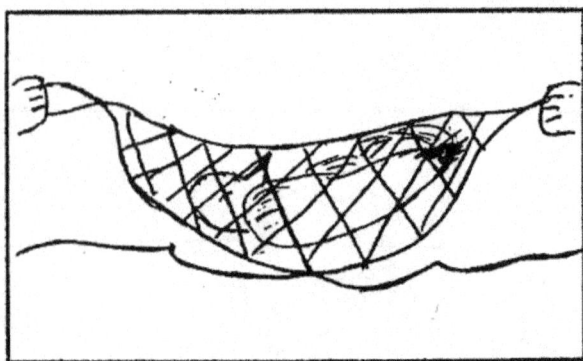

Gill the gull fell! Gill fell in a net. The gull can not get up.

The men pick up the net. Tug, rip and the men send Gill up. Gill did a zig and a zag.

8

Pug ran with a wag. The men pet Pug. Pug tends the sub and Gill can not sit on the sub.

Gill will not sit on the hull. Gill the gull will sit on the sand.

THE

END

THE

END

SHORT VOWELS
With digraphs ch, sh, and wh
and being verbs
Through Lesson 35

The

Chums

a   e   i   o   u

am   is   are

was   were

has   have   had

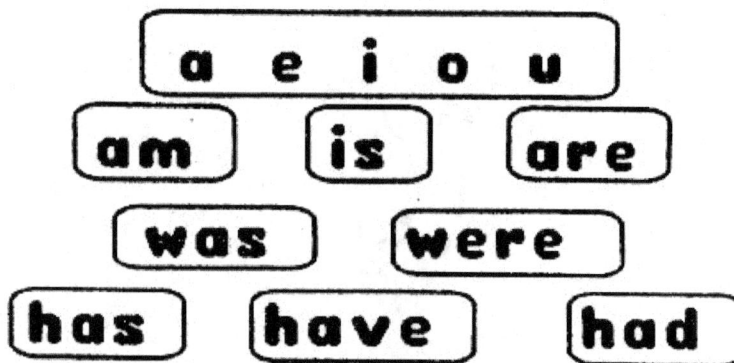

Written and Illustrated by
Barbara Simkus

Published by
The Paradigm Company
3500 Mountain View Dr. Boise, ID, 83704

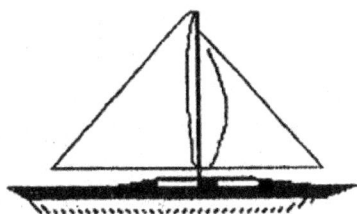

Chuck and his chum, Chet, had a ship.

They put the ship in at the pond. Chuck and Chet push and the ship shot off.

Chuck, with a rush, ran and got it when the ship hit land.

Back at Chet he will push it.

1

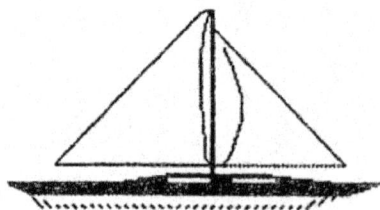

What fun!

Chet did a dash. Will he get

the ship?

A big rock was in his path.

Chet fell and hit his chin.

That was a shock!

Chuck ran. Such a mess!

Chuck fell and hit his shin.

Chuck gets up and runs to

Chet.

Chet has a big gash in his chin.

Chuck and Chet rush back for mom.

Mom has a wash rag and put it on Chet's chin.

"Hush, Hush," mom tells them. It is not bad and she will fix it. Mom is quick and Chet did not fuss. Chuck did not have a gash. Mom will wash his leg and hug him.

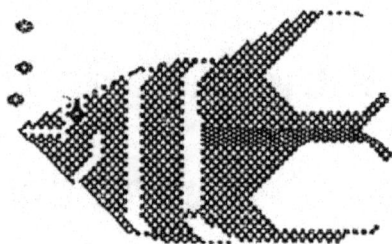

Then Chuck and Chet will
shop with mom.

Chuck and Chet have a bit of
cash. Chuck is set to get a
fish.

Which fish will he get? The
red one he tells Chet.

Chet will get a mesh net for

the fish.

They shop and shop. The Fish

Shack has no red fish.

Chip's Fish Shop has red fish!

The one with the big fins is

the one Chuck gets.

Chet gets a shell to put in

with the fish.

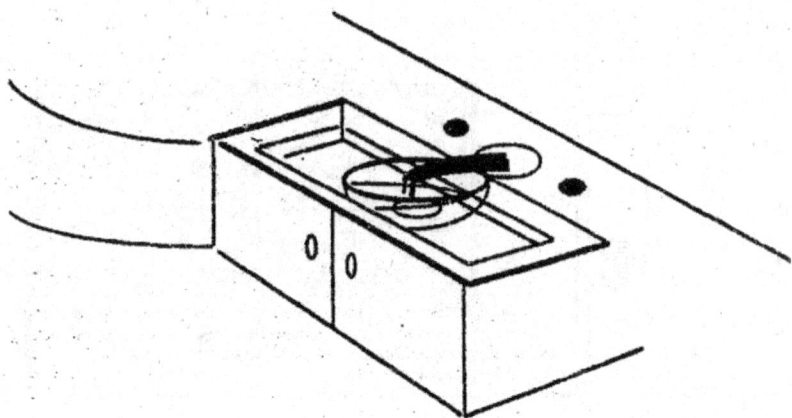

Mom, Chuck and Chet hop in
the van. They are back.
"Quick," mom tells Chuck and
Chet, "the fish can not get a
chill." They rush in.
"Pick a big dish," mom tells
them. Chuck gets a big one
and they fill it up.

6

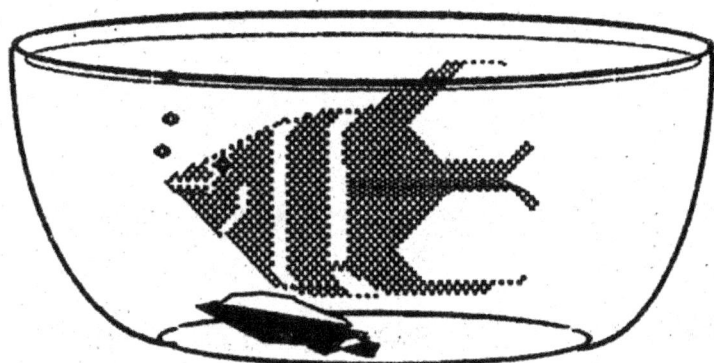

Chet gets his net.

In the dish dips the net with
the fish.

Zip! Zag! Zig! and the fish
is off.

They put the shell in with the
fish. Phil the fish is fun.

Chuck and Chet are chums.

Dad is back. They tell him
that Chet has a gash and that
Chuck has a nob on his shin.
Dad will be with them at the
pond. "Get the ship and we will
have fun," dad tells them.
Chet will push the ship to
Chuck and then Chuck will
push it to Chet.
Chums til the end.

SHORT VOWELS
Through Lesson 42

VELVET
THE
TOMCAT

Written and Illustrated by
Barbara Simkus

Published by
The Paradigm Company
3500 Mountain View Dr. Boise, ID, 83704

Velvet is a tomcat. He sits in

the sun and naps.

Then Velvet gets up and hops in

a box. Zing! He runs and bats

the boxtop.

Cal puts a ping-pong ball in the

box. Pop, bop, Velvet hits the

ball.

Zip! Zap! and Velvet is off to the basket. Then he runs up the hatrack.

Ding-Dong! A bell rings. Cal will get it. A man with a ten-gallon hat is let in. He hangs his hat on the rack. Cal calls dad.

The man and dad will sit in the den. They get the chess set.

Velvet is on the hatrack.

Wack! He pushes the ten-gallon hat off. Mash! Velvet is on the hat.

BAT! BAT! BOP! The hat hits the wall. Wack, wack and the hat is up. Bat, hit, zap, the hat is in the hall.

Hop, and Velvet is in the hat.

Bap, bat, rip! Sock! The cat

and the hat are in the den.

Velvet can't get off the hat.

He hops and he pulls. Then he

backs up....BAM!

The cactus falls. Dad and the

man are up and rush at Velvet.

Zip, and Velvet shot off. Push,

Push, he is upset.

Back, back, Velvet runs.

He can't get off the hat.

Up he hops and back! Gong!

Bong! The chess set falls.

Dad and the man pick up Velvet

with the hat.

Dad pulls the hat

and Velvet didn't fuss.

5

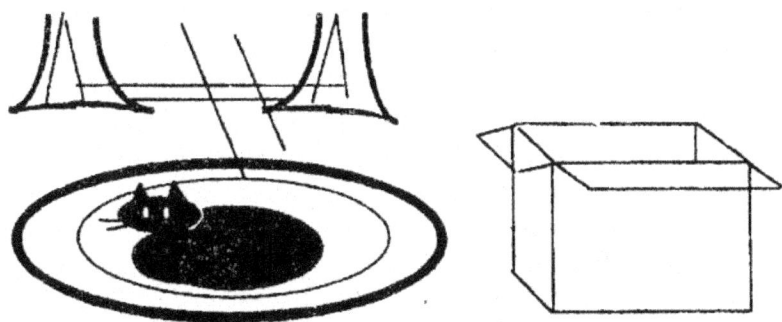

The hat is a mess. Dad tells

Velvet, "You are a bad cat!

What a rascal."

Dad tells the man, "Let's get

you a hat at the hat shop."

Velvet runs and sits on the rug

in the sun.

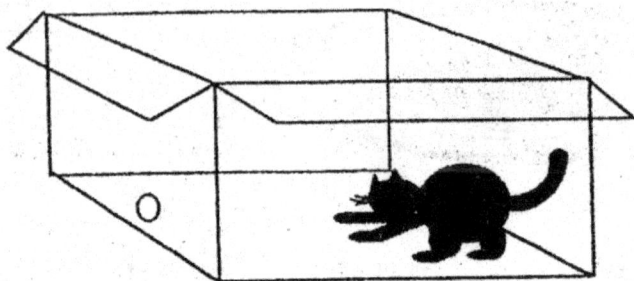

Velvet will quit running and

getting dad upset.

He will have the ping-pong ball

in the box and bat at it.

The sun on the rug is hot.

Velvet will sing a cat song as

he naps in the sun.

SHORT
VOWELS
MIXED
Covers lessons up to 49

THE
BIG
FISH

Written and Illustrated by
Barbara Simkus

Published by
The Paradigm Company
3500 Mountain View Dr.   Boise, ID, 83704

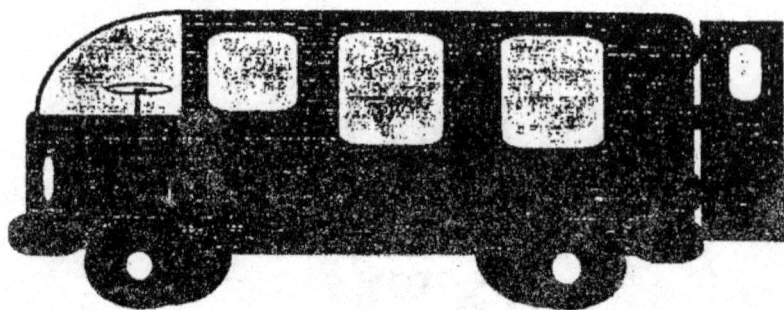

Bill is ten. Dad and Bill are fixing the tent. They will have fun fishing and tenting at Bob's Pond.

Dad tells Bill, "First we will put the tent in back of the van. Then you can put the fishing rods in the van."

1

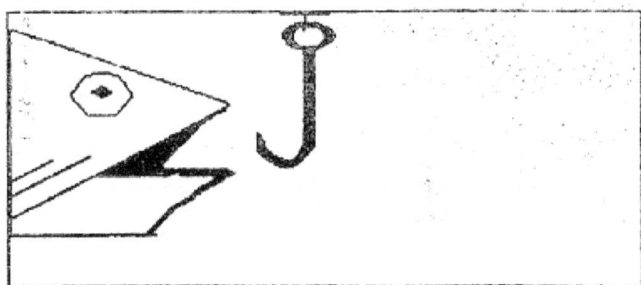

"What did you put the bobbers

in?" Bill asks dad. "They are

in the box."

Then Bill asks, "Can I have

one when we are fishing?"

"Yes," dad tells him.

Bill puts the tent, the box and

the rods in the van.

Dad and Bill are all packed.

They get in the van. Honk!

Honk! They are off.

Not much traffic and past

the long bend is Bob's

ranch.

Dad and Bill are at the

ranch at dusk. Bob is bigger

than dad and picks up Bill

and hugs him.

"You are getting big," Bob
tells Bill.

Dad asks Bob if he can put the tent on the sand at the pond.

"The best land is west of the pond," Bob tells them.

"Well, let's get that tent up and have a chat," Dad tells them.

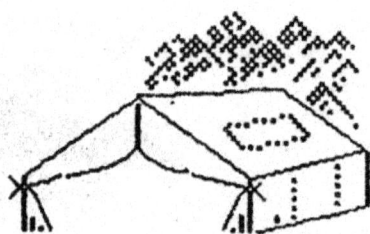

Dad, Bob, and Bill get the
tent. They set up the tent
and chat a bit.

Dad wants rest. Bill puts
the mats and the bags in the
tent.

Dad and Bill get in the bags
and nod off til sun-up.

Bill is up and mist is on the pond.

Dad has ham and eggs in the pan.

"We must get the fishing rods," Dad tells Bill.

Bill is off and gets the rods.

He is back and has ham and eggs. "The best ham and eggs, yet," Bill jests.

Bill wants to fish but Dad
must wash the pan first.
Then Dad yells, "Let's
fish!"
"Let's test the rods, Bill.
Pick it up and cast," Dad
tells Bill. Bill lifts his rod
up and pops it fast.
"You did well Bill and you
can get a bobber ." Bill is
fishing and that is fun.

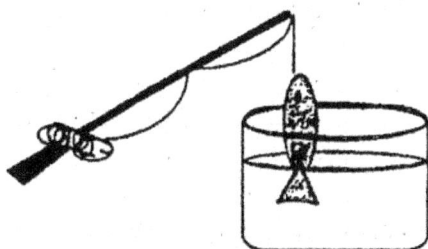

The sun is hot on the mist.

They fish and fish.

Bill has a big tug on his
rod.

Pull, pull, and next Bill has

a big fish.

What a big fish! They can't

get it in the net. Dad will

put it in the gallon can.

8

Bob and his son, Jack, are at
the tent. "Call Bob and
Jack and tell them we have a
big fish," Bill tells Dad.
Dad yells and calls Bob and
Jack.
Next, they are all fishing.
Dad,Bob and Jack get lots of
fish. But not one of them
gets a fish as big as Bill's
fish.

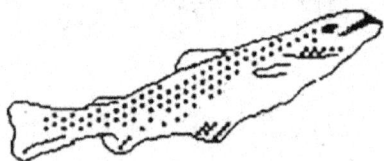

9

Back at the tent they put the fish in a pan but Bill's fish is not one of them.

Bill will put his fish in the van.

When he hands Mom the fish she will have a big hug and kiss for Bill.

Short Vowel
Reader
Through Lesson 57

THE

CONTEST

Written and Illustrated by
Barbara Simkus

Published by
The Paradigm Company
3500 Mountain View Dr.   Boise, ID, 83704

Pam and Peg are pals. They
sing in the "Chapel Gang".
All the kids in the "Gang"
have fun when they sing.

They will all sing at the
Camp Ledge Contest.

Pam is bashful and Peg isn't.

Peg talks a lot and Pam can't.

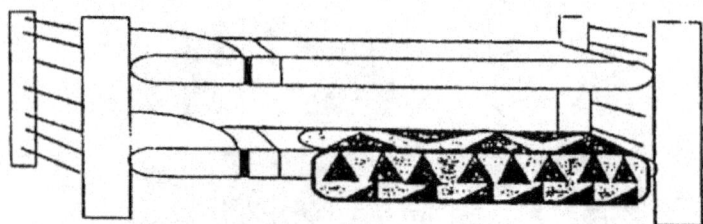

At Camp Ledge they have bunk beds. Pam has the top bunk. Peg has a quilt on her bunk.

They will rest a bit and then they will sing at ten.

As they sit on the bunks, they sing the songs.

"Let's quit," Pam tells Peg.

"Since when are you a
quitter?" Peg asks.

"I am not but I wish I was not
bashful," Pam tells Peg.

"Just sing and ask Jesus to
help you and He will," Peg
tells Pam.

Pam and Peg must walk up the
hill. The lodge is on top of
the hill.

All of the "Gang" is in the
lodge. They will sing six
songs.

Pam and Peg must sing a
song. Pam is tense.

Pam asks Jesus for help. Pam
is not tense after that and
sings her best.

Peg has a puppet and it talks.

Peg can have it dance and

sing.

Patch the puppet is a big hit.

This is the last act.

Can the "Chapel Gang" win

the contest?

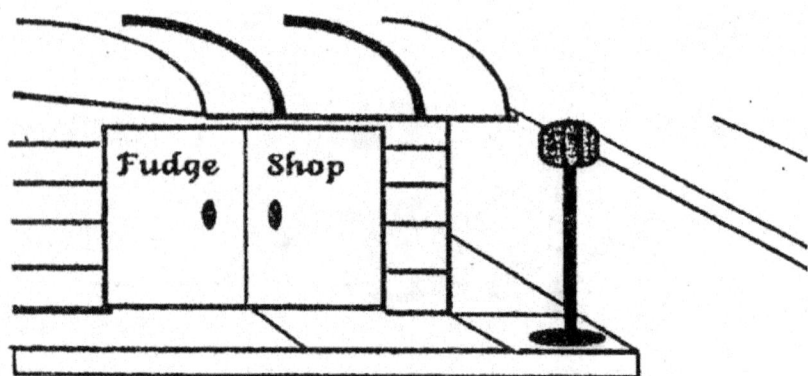

The judges are back.

The "Gang wins the contest.

They all jump up and yell.

Next Pam, Peg and the

"Gang" have a sandwich,

chips and milk.

Then they are all off and visit

a fudge shop. Yummmm!

After all the fun, the "Gang" gets on the bus. Pam and Peg sit back and rest. They all had fun.

The End

SHORT VOWEL READER
Through Lesson 71

Silly
Sentences
II

Written by
Barbara Simkus

Published by
The Paradigm Company
3500 Mountain View Dr. Boise, ID, 83704

Blend the black blot on the blond blank block.

Bring the brass brush back.

He had bran on the brink of the brick bridge.

A clod, a clob, a clump and a clock clattered off the cliff.

The class will clamp the clasp and the clip on the clan's club.

The crass crank will crush the crop.

Drop the drab dress.

Don't drip the drink on the drill.

Fran, Frank and
Fred did not fret.

The fresh frost was
on the French frog.

Flip the flat flap,
Flash!

The flock fled as
the flag flapped.

Greg had a glad grin.

Grab the glass, Gwen.

In the grass of the grand glen was a glut of glum grubs.

Grant held a grim grudge.

The prince did plot and plan.

Plop a plucked plum
on a plank.

The prim prince was
prompt.

The sled slid on the
slick slush.

Slim slid the slab on
a slant.

The smell of the
smog smacked of
small shrimp.

Spell — spill, spit,
spot, spat and spud.

The spring sprang
and spun til spent.

Stick the stiff strip
of string on the
stack of straps.

The stag will strut,
step and stomp.

The swift swan will
swim the swamp.

The skunk will skip
with skill.

The trek of the
trash truck with the
trunk tricked us.

Twelve twitching thushes throb and thrill the throng

The
End

Little Companion Readers Series

These readers were designed to be used with *Alpha-Phonics* - A Primer for Beginning Readers and *How To Tutor* by Samuel L. Blumenfeld. It is possible to use them with any phonics program that starts with short vowels and progresses to long vowels.

When the child has completed the lessons for a particular vowel, let them read the book.

Short Vowel A - Silly Sentences

Short Vowel E - The Hen and The Pen

Short Vowel I - Tim the Pig

Short Vowel 0 - The Mill

Short Vowel U - Pug the Pup

Short Vowels with digraphs sh, ch, wh - The Chums (How To tutor lesson 23]

Short Vowels - Velvet the Tomcat
[Alpha-Phonics lesson 42, How To Tutor lesson 31]

Short Vowels - The Big Fish
[Alpha-Phonics lesson 49, How To Tutor lesson 49]

Short Vowels - The Contest
[Alpha-Phonics lesson 57]

Short Vowels - Silly Sentences II
[Alpha-Phonics lesson 71, How To Tutor lesson 63]

www.ingramcontent.com/pod-product-compliance
Lightning Source LLC
LaVergne TN
LVHW021525080426